Melody the Monkey
and
The U.S. Presidents

Written and Composed by
Deborah E. Benner-Davis

Illustrated by
Evalee McBean
and
Deborah E. Benner-Davis

Second Edition

For
Family members and others
who have served our country

Melody left school one day singing as she often did. She loved to sing.

She had just learned a new song in school that she wanted to make sure that she did not forget called "The U.S. Presidents".

Just then her friend Eager the Eagle flew by. "What are you singing?", he asked.

"I am singing about the presidents of the United States. Do you know them all?", Melody asked.

"Of course," he said. "I am a bald eagle the national symbol and bird of the United States."

9

Melody asked Eager if he wanted to sing with her.

"I would love to sing with you," Eager replied.

They both laughed and began to sing.

Here are the presidents of the United States of America.

(Music written on page 46)

10

1 - George Washington
1789-1797

2 - John Adams
1797-1801

3 - Thomas Jefferson
1801-1809

and then comes

4 - James Madison
1809-1817

5 - James Monroe
1817-1825

6 - John Quincy Adams
1825-1829

Yes, he's the son!

7 - Andrew Jackson
1829-1837

8 - Martin Van Buren
1837-1841

16

9 - William H. Harrison
1841

10 - John Tyler
1841-1845

11 - James K. Polk
1845-1849

and then comes

**12 - Zachary Taylor
1849-1850**

**13 - Millard Fillmore
1850-1853**

19

14 - Franklin Pierce
1853-1857

and then comes

15 - James Buchanan
1857-1861

16 - Abraham Lincoln
1861-1865

17 - Andrew Johnson
1865-1869

18 - Ulysses S. Grant
1869-1877

19 - Rutherford B. Hayes
1877-1881

20 - James A. Garfield
1881

21 - Chester A. Arthur
1881-1885

24

22 - Grover Cleveland
1885-1889

and then comes

23 - Benjamin Harrison
1889-1893

24 - Grover Cleveland
1893-1897

yes, it's him again!

and then comes

25 - William McKinley
1897-1901

26 - Theodore Roosevelt
1901-1909

27 - William H. Taft
1909-1913

28 - Woodrow Wilson
1913-1921

29 - Warren G. Harding
1921-1923

30 - Calvin Coolidge
1923-1929

31 - Herbert C. Hoover
1929-1933

32 - Franklin D. Roosevelt
1933-1945

and then comes

**33 - Harry S. Truman
1945-1953**

**34 - Dwight D. Eisenhower
1953-1961**

35 - John F. Kennedy
1961-1963

and then comes

36 - Lyndon B. Johnson
1963-1969

37 - Richard M. Nixon
1969-1974

38 - Gerald R. Ford
1974-1977

39 - Jimmy Carter
1977-1981

40 - Ronald Reagan
1981-1989

41 - George H.W. Bush
1989-1993

42 - William "Bill" Clinton
1993-2001

Now let's see who's next!

and then comes

43 - George W. Bush
2001-2009
Yes, he is the son!

44 - Barrack Obama
2009-2017

and then comes

45 - Donald J. Trump
2017-2021

46 - Joe Biden
2021-2025

47 - Donald J. Trump
2025-

yes, it's him again!

That's all for now...

**We have to wait to see
who is next?**

When they finished singing, both Melody and Eager the Eagle laughed.

Eager reminded Melody that they would be able to add more presidents to the song as more presidents were elected. They would have to wait at least four years from the last election to do that.

They waved goodbye to each other as they both went on their way. Both were still singing about the U.S. Presidents.

45

Tips for Parents:

1. To help children memorize the Presidents, repeat and echo works the best - Start with you singing first and then they repeat each name.

When they start to learn the names, sing two or three names at a time and then have them repeat. Then do as verses.

(Recording of the song is also located on the website. The song can also be done as a rap.)

2. President's Day - 3rd Monday of February celebrates George Washington's & Abraham Lincoln's birthdays.

3. Theordore and Franklin Roosevelt were related as well. They were distant cousins. (Three sets of relations - Roosevelts, Adams, and Bushes)

4. 1st black president - Barack Obama

Tips for Parents:

5. 1st physically disabled president - Franklin D. Roosevelt

6. It is possible for anyone to be president.

7. What year is it now? When is the next election?

8. The dates the presidents held office and which number they were numerically to help with the start of U.S. history.

9. Which presidents are on U.S. currency? and what denomination of money?

10. Which presidents did not serve two terms in a row?

The U.S. Presidents

Words and Music by
Deborah E. Benner-Davis

48

Also by Deborah E. Benner-Davis:

Melody the Monkey's Musical Alphabet
Melody the Monkey and Angry the Alligator
Melody the Monkey and Buzzy the Bee
Melody the Monkey and Cozy the Cat
Melody the Monkey and Dashing the Dog
Melody the Monkey and Fancy the Fish
Melody the Monkey and Eager the Eagle
Melody the Monkey and Greedy the Gorilla
Melody the Monkey's Animal Rap

Visit www.melodythemonkey.org
for free parent information, crafts, activities,
videos, contact information and more.

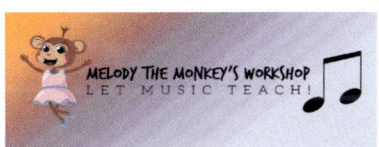

Change the World Through Music!
Children Are Our Future!
Let's Give Them Every Opportunity!
Melody the Monkey's Workshop is a non-profit that
empowers all children including the underprivileged,
very young and special needs to learn through music
by giving them even more educational tools for life-
long learning and benefits children's programs.

20538990R00029